HER NOT ALL HER

ELFRIEDE JELINEK

Her Not All Her
on/with Robert Walser

*Translated from the
German by Damion Searls*

The Cahiers
Series

CENTER FOR WRITERS & TRANSLATORS
THE AMERICAN UNIVERSITY OF PARIS

—

SYLPH EDITIONS

A number of people to each other, all very friendly
and well-behaved (perhaps lying in bathtubs,
as was once the custom in mental hospitals)

Moment, bleiben Sie stehen!
WAIT, DON'T SIT DOWN! Your soul is peeping out of
your body as though a work lay there inside you like a
slumbering goddess, wanting to get out, even in her sleep. That's
how it seems to me at least. Things that peep forth often annoy
people who want to be forthright themselves. This soul, then, has
a nice stretch inside you, as though what it wanted was to become
language but then never have anything to do with itself again.
Certainly nothing like getting away from your body! Now here
is where you pass away, relieved. Someone out for a walk, with
ideas and inspirations trailing after him so that again and again
he has to stop and listen to check if anyone is treading underfoot
this hem of his soul. So he can free it faster. That's what makes
a person hem, as well as haw! This ambling along with blinded
eyes that nonetheless still have to look into the light is not right
for a goddess, who, after all, even when she looks off-putting, with
water flowing from her eyes, can only ever remain herself. And no
one expects anything else from her. Or do they? Your work, my
dear sir, is quite strange! The fewer steps you take on the road
to yourself the faster you end up beside yourself, is how I see
it. Right, the writer goes forth from himself and then right away
goes right away from himself, old and decrepit; he can only bring
someone else to life, never revive himself. He unfurls his human
nature and it turns into another nature, then into entire natural
features in whose chasms it's easy to get lost. Now who does the
writer mean by himself? His goddess briefly appears in Western
thought, examines her fingernails most assiduously, then rushes
off again. Oh really, a goddess is going to do your work for you
and pierce the raw husk of your exterior at last? My goodness,
she's a real vulture, suddenly picking at the fried liver on your
plate! Not all that has glittery wings and hurts to look at (or: not
everyone whom looking hurts) is a goddess. And even if they all
are, yours isn't! These beings, yours and your creation's, are often
mistaken for each other, alas. Then one day you are no longer

afraid of the bigger one, which was lurking inside you the whole time, since when it comes out it annoyingly turns very small, so small that no one would think it worth closer inspection. Or is it only making itself seem small? Cringing because silence rings out so loud now and those who are fated to die really do?

WHAT, THAT'S THE GODDESS? There she goes, a peculiar apparition. Path and forest floor resemble a carpet. Here in the middle of the forest it is silent, as in the happy human soul from which the work has emerged, or in a temple, or a magic castle, or dreamlike fairy-tale palaces like Sleeping Beauty's, where everything sleeps and stays silent down through the long centuries. Instead it's now the work that speaks! But no, your work doesn't speak in your stead! Well anyway, where were we? Was there anything we forgot to mention about the solemnity of the forest? You wait and hope for years and years and in two minutes it's all over, unless it's a Mozart aria, then it lasts ten. It was all rehearsed, yes, the writer nurses his childhood and when he wakes all wake with him, they waken within him, they burst their locks and start to glow with glowering melancholy over having been woken. They think that they've lost something in their sleep. You can focus on musicality but it won't help. Music is always a stranger on this earth, but the disadvantage of language is that it can all too quickly seem familiar and so you throw it off, horrified, as though you'd touched something disgusting. Do you understand what I'm saying? So, these ten minutes of Mozart crowd in, one minute stumbling into the other until they all fall down together, into this here for instance, the woman next to me, a shop-girl maybe twenty-four years old who has never heard such sounds or anything like them and, believe it or not, these sounds that have her by the throat draw forth tears of enchantment that were sealed up inside her, large and pure, the whole time. Now music has been brought to bear and it can be gathered up like little flowers, or eaten, like spicy sausage, salad, and roast potatoes. But what does language make happen? Language is worth as little as life itself, for it is life itself.

LIFE. Now mine for example is worthy of a novel! Would you like to hear the novel of my life? For that I'd need to think long

and hard first. I have it inside me, true, but while I'm thinking I can't talk. Nor while I eat or sleep, that's not allowed either. Then when? Well, for whatever reason, it doesn't (what's inside me) come out. Sometimes it's also because my door says 'Occupied', which I often don't notice in those first eager moments. You can see the sign only from outside, so to speak, but it's from inside that you have to slide back the bolt so that you can finally get entirely outside yourself. If you ventured out, though, you would be stronger in character and in the idiosyncracies you could then attribute to others who are utterly innocent of them, in fact they often would not even know how many or few I had apportioned to them. Yes, I am happy to loan out my flame to this spirit! Oh dear, it's gone out! And so we see that nothing is certain in this world of ours, wracked by storms and afflictions. All, all is weak. All my shame all around, across the landscape! Really the only reason I write is so as not to have to deal with myself! Shadows

Ich schreibe ja nur, um den Umgang mit mir zu vermeiden!

made real and then made over to others. My silence sounds in their ears. No, wait a minute! I can't say it audibly after all. Traipse around softly inside me, ferret out intellectual words for me to repudiate again, full of emotion; fear the coincidence of another author possibly having found exactly the same thing I did to still the stillness inside him at last; well all right, now even the most harmless things call out to me even though I did not expect their call in the least, and already I'm rubbing words against each other like a cricket its wings. Oh dear, now I've created a beast of prey like Mr. Strindberg! I am so infinitely sorry! It's in order to seem wild and voracious like that that people think up such things and let them speak for them, cowards as they are. Some of them would be sincere enough to talk, it's true, but very few of them could actually answer for themselves. They are no beasts of prey, more like in between. When a tiger thinks it has no chance to be a tiger, it wants to turn into a sheep at once, whether from irritation or nostalgia. By which I mean: Everyone should make himself as small as he possibly can. That should certainly apply to me too, no question about it. I am not making fun of the somnolent. But I myself am always wide awake. Something is spoken so that you can make yourself believe that something is slinking in you like a tiger. But only depicting tiger or sheep with a single word was allowed. And as soon as someone pulls out a yardstick to lay

alongside what has been created, suddenly it no longer works
to be a beast of prey.

BE SATISFIED WITH THE SIMPLEST CIRCUMSTANCES in your
life, for in systematic order lies the greatest beauty! Even when
assiduously dissipating yourself, a certain tidying up still needs
to happen within you, later at the latest, if only in case you want
to collect yourself. Why is it that natures which embody peace
and understanding and good will are in general only glanced at in
passing and consequently all too easily, in fact always, esteemed as
slight, namely as compared to those inclined to get tempests and
raging intensities going? If you unfurl your modest little charm
and then shamefacedly furl it up again – as fluttering butterflies
do, always looking around beforehand to see if anyone has
discovered their butterfly essence – then you'll never stand out.
And after decking your wings in such beautiful colours, especially
for the occasion! Surely not just so you could be overlooked at the
last minute! Then again, colours too can signify order, warlike
armour, golden hair, a bird making its cheery voice heard from
its charming, holy hiding place. All that only so that someone
will look at us affectionately. Of course he does so, we realise too
late, only to judge us as severely as possible. So. The judgment
is spoken, the stranger sinks, loaded down as he is by the hot
flames of a spirit, flushed out of a burning building. Later all is in
order again.

Das Urteil ist gesprochen, das Fremde geht unter, beladen wie es ist von den heißen Flammen eines Geistes, aufgejagt aus einem brennenden Haus.

THINGS WERE TIDIED UP especially for you. This order is also the
reason why you never leave your circle of friends any more even
though they have long since known all the prejudices and personal
interests you have your eye on. You have described them a
hundred times already. All the lines are now stowed away safe and
silent inside you like dead bodies. Even now there is life enough
in most of us if only we give ourselves time to find ourselves! So
why don't your thoughts want to come out any more? Mine do,
but only to pile up on sheets of paper, stubborn and disappointing.
Yours probably can't as well as mine can. Mine practically fizz
triumphantly, alas always toward the end of the occasions when
I'm sitting in jolly company, and as soon as everything is at its
most fun everyone stands up at the same time to take their leave.

And yours? Yours have dragged themselves inside you and there they then end before they can get back out again. No one grieves with you for what you were not able to say. You have the following flaws: You go for a walk with a dog that busily clatters along the road with its paws, you stroll and thereby spread what is most well known, what's easiest, but then you immediately start to slip over the line into the realm of the questionable, always without asking where this line of thought might have led. No light at the end. So even the questionable doesn't get you to ask questions. Writers, not unlike generals, often make the most tedious preparations before they proceed to the attack and bravely deliver their battles. Don't leave your weapons at home all the time! Are you doing it on purpose? From the art of poetry war has arisen: People were bored by what they knew but they didn't want to ask anything either. They wanted to answer right off. But there's one thing they know for certain: always conquer new ground! That's what it means to be an artist! These things take time. The great man from Salzburg simply invented his cheerful melodies with the help of his cheerful nature and now we Europeans look back on a thousand-year-old culture and ask ourselves: Was that really necessary? Well, let's take away ten years, no one will notice and it won't make the culture any smaller. We'll use those ten years in our own life, but that won't make our life any bigger either, which is something the cleverer sorts know in advance, so they don't even try to do anything with life. Anyway, what I'd really want to do is learn how to live, whereas others direct their efforts to living a little longer than usual. It is a happy man who does not know a thing about what it means to be alone. Wanderer, come quietly in! A stranger dies after not having spoken for twenty-three years. He preferred to count peas and try to wrap himself up in tin-foil like a present, but then, after all that, no one wanted him. Come, you creators, making notes on paper, letters of the alphabet! Bring on the incessant undisturbedness needed to do

Hier wird anständig geschwiegen!

so! Here silence is respectably kept. Well, now your ten years have passed too. Ten years should certainly have been enough, my dear little peacemaker!

SO WHY ALL THIS BLUBBERING? What are you scattering there like seeds? What brings you hurrying hither with the other

women writers of note – where does your memory point? It can't
point at a place you've never been to! Now don't be reckless and
point to a place you haven't explored, otherwise you might have
to stay there and the natives believed to have died out might eat
you! People come up to you, along a snowy path, and seem at first
sight to be seeing the unseeable. As though their rowboat were
sinking under sufferings. Quick, pick up your hat! If you don't,
someone else will step on it too. There is simply no way for you
to file a complaint, the feeling is mutual and you certainly don't
want to hear the other side! Please, Sir, ward off the shadows
of the other side that has turned its back on you! Someone over
there, to keep his lordly nature in line and make it wait patiently,
tells it: I like dancing, and the food tastes delicious, and life itself is
like a dove or a swallow flying up from somewhere or another that
always swerves away from my mouth at the last possible moment.

Sie werden mich in mir nicht finden, aber Sie
ARE YOU LOOKING FOR ME? You won't find me in me, but if
können mich, wenn Sie sich auf die Vorderbeine niederlassen, gern besichtigen!
you go down on one knee you're welcome to look me over! I am
low to the ground like flowers, which are also able to move only
in limited ways and with the help of a gentle breeze. The thing is,
I too am locked up inside myself and cannot recover from myself
in, for instance, a coffeehouse. It's nice to stand around in train
stations too, where I can comfortably observe the travellers, both
those arriving and those continuing on. You have travelled such
a long way to get to know me, but alas I must inform you that
every loudspeaker announcing departure times knows more about
me and my destinations than I do. Travellers intending to board
tell me such things. Not that they're really interested in me. I'm
happy to see them off anyway. My bodily form is already pursing
its lips to give them a kiss, but all that happens is that something
I ate falls out. All the better. Today, once again, no one has let
me depict them with syllables, words, and lines. Once again, no
one has welcomed me with open hands and arms. Maybe I go
right past people too fast with all my requests. It must be almost
unpleasant for them at times, to know that they possess such and
such value, since they would then have to grant me almost exactly
the same value too! The only thing they don't begrudge me is that
the lamps in my room work and cast a beautiful image of evening
onto the wall. But then night comes with all its endlessness,

everyone goes to sleep, and all the grace of the day that was handed over to them to keep vanishes without a trace in my, yes, my self-surrender. I climb of my own free will into the box and lie down. Make myself small. Not a word about me strikes anyone. And the words that have come to me, the foundling, I found somewhere else. They insisted they all went together. That led right to an attempt to awaken self-awareness. Soon red filled the sky and now I'm already starting up again with shovelling in food. I constantly lack something, I am in its ghostly track. I am intractable. Oh, no, it wasn't food I was missing, nor the taking of walks. There's no point. I enter into every circle and then again none. From time to time a strict attendant chases me but it's no skin off my back, after all I've seen something beautiful again with my own eyes!

THE PEOPLE YOU SHARE YOUR LIFE WITH, Sir, make you stupid and impoverished with their presence. Piece by piece they take away every inspiration you have. And now you give the impression of knowing absolutely nothing. Don't worry, I'll save you the boring search, I'll look for myself myself, in fact I've been doing so for years in order to gain recognition in a rather unfriendly way, in contrast to you. I am so precious and important that I would never entrust this search to anyone else, especially not to a writer. So if I'm already looking for myself you do not have to do anything further in that regard. I will find myself much faster than you could, since of course as a rule I know where I am. But sometimes I do have to conclude that I am not at home in myself! And in fact it doesn't matter to me where else I might *Und es ist mir sogar egal, wo ich sonst sein könnte.* be. Maybe I'm busily living on somewhere else, until I die. I am especially defenceless against you whenever I have once more failed to find myself in time. Then difficulties appear in my path, and with a powerful effort to move (with both feet! no running start!) I make it off the path and can't find my way back home. No one touches me as I meander around, since of course they don't know either where I am going to stop. I am constantly being touched by something that doesn't see me and sometimes even passes right through me. My defenceless staying out means *Meine Schutzlosigkeit bedeutet den* goodbye income, means the persistence of matter and the circling *Abschied von jedem Bezug, bedeutet das Ständige der Gegenstände und das* of circumference and the filtering of the entity. I could give you *Umkreisen des Umkreises und das Duchseihen des Seienden.*

a clue to hang on to: that I am sitting in the streetcar where you,
too, could easily hang on to the strap next to me, if you want,
I have nothing against that. There's something free to hang on to
right here. This mate of mine is somewhere else at every moment.
And you too seem to be going to look for me somewhere else. Are
you waiting? What, won't you stop seeking me? Stop! I hereby
free you from my unfreedom! I allow you to be well in your
well-being! You're welcome to be, as far as I'm concerned. It's
my fault! I am putting a slip of paper for you here on the kitchen
table with the information that I am on my way to you, in public
view all around, around the roundabout where I rush to vanish
from thought again. I won't put down roots where I'm driving
to. I am invariably nimbly off again before anyone can figure me
out. And I speak of deep things, for all the lifecycle-lane signs on
the roundabout all around me trying to slow my traffic. They
show me the exits I can take, but I miss them at the last minute.
No, my depth doesn't reach its limits. No one should try to pour
depths into something as shallow as me! Obviously I could go
Man sollte eben nicht Tiefes in etwas so Seichtes wie mich einzufüllen versuchen!
somewhere else too. In contrast, as always, to a plant, which has
to stay where it is, or dies if someone pulls it up. Some plants
are scared, I'm sure of it, when they push their way up out of
the ground and meet, precisely there, someone, for instance the
hand of someone bent over, bent over by life and nothing but.
Somewhere else someone reads about me and cries, as though
he had nothing better to do. He has chosen, of course, a choice,
especially touching place to read and believes for the moment
that it's his, his place, but in fact he has long since lost his place.
I would not want to be in his place, since it's gone now. Occupied
by someone else, most likely.

IS YOUR ROOM AS THIN AS MINE? Why has it lost so much
weight? I was given permission to take the key whenever I wanted,
but I don't do it. I let them unlock the door for me, for I am
content with the hope that I might return healthy from this outing
or excursion into the cheerless zone of the diseased. But whenever
I come back after adventures bravely met and overcome, I am sick
if only because the train that passes through the place where I am
several times a day once again did not have the courtesy to pass
scrupulously past. It stopped, as always, inside me, as though I and

my ticket were supposed to be checked, by you. I don't know you.
Have we met? Maybe somewhere on one of these ice-encrusted
highways and byways of reading? Here was a book, there a brook,
and again I was introduced to a beautiful, distinguished woman
to whom I felt attracted. I could write about her right away, except
I only write about what I feel, or hear, or ideas I have. Alas, I did
not have the idea to grasp the cool, slender fingers of this lady's
hand until it was too late. I ask out loud: Is it true? Am I all the *Laut frage ich: Ist es wahr? Bin ich Ihnen gleichgültig?*
same to you? Don't you care? She looks darkly at the space before
her, sulks, and is angry. Her mouth, a true dumping ground for
every variety of contempt, twists into a bitter smile. I am fooling
myself. My room is the only one with the power to caress me with
its spatial effects. Only here do I feel in good hands. Every other
room would just leave me lying there forgotten, has often done
so of course and perhaps even trampled upon me rather than
helping me to my feet. But not this little fella. This one even lets
me, needy as I am, go out into the forest whenever I want, under
a dripping fir tree, to the friendly houses, through a carolling of
birds, into the most beautiful sunset! I like to appear unspeakably
happy in my room and I can do it too. Similarly, I would basically
not have had anything to reproach all the other rooms in the
world with, even if they were located in a forest, on the highest
mountain, or on the water, but this much is true: None of my
previous rooms helped me. They refused me their sleeves with
which I might perhaps have been able to keep myself and my poor
face covered. No one should expect too much from anyone else.
I, for example: no matter how clearly it is given me to understand
that I am obliged to give much, I give nothing, I just don't really
want to. Only this one room, this last room, already so totally
saturated with me and yet notoriously satisfied with me, still
gives me succour. It's possible that all the other rooms, every time
I needed them, already had claims on them from elsewhere.

IT USED TO BE THAT not even my rooms could so much as feel
my presence, and they knew me really quite well. Always knew
when I was there. To this one room, the last, I must, however,
make one small reproach, the last: Shouldn't it have suspected
something and held me back when I wanted to go out into
the snow? I am, it is true, an avid walker, I even take walks on

Christmas Day. Why should my room have had any suspicions
this time? It welcomes me back in on good days, while I continue
to raise the objections fetched forth from the being of my
memory – but this was a bad day. Memory is thought! But who
remembers death? No one can do that. No, this time this room
did not take me in, perhaps because I myself had taken too much
in and, immoderate as I sometimes am, had stuffed myself full
of it, until suddenly it was more than I could bear. This freight
elevator has a maximum capacity of two persons, the reader and
the well-read, and these two cannot bear any additional weight
without disturbing the course of things, which have, after all,
been taking their course for a while now. Memory, from which
I create, is therefore death, treacherous as a mineshaft. Memory
presents itself as part of a creature's fundamental equipment
and thus as the most human thing there is, since people always
have to convene gatherings, preferably in themselves, and it is
their memories that are supposed to come by this afternoon
for tea. But gatherings are not to be confused with assemblies,
there you give something of yourself, here you take something
in. Suddenly we had five hundred people here, and more, no,
not one more, since you can no longer count on me! Memory
assembles remembrances, luckily many of them were cheap
or cost absolutely nothing. But suddenly we're ashamed at the
sight of them and hide them away again, the greetings that none
shall receive except the most foreign stranger of all, the wanderer
Mancher
who rises up before us today in front of the house. Some may
würde meine Worte in die Strafkolonie einer Dichtung stecken und
throw my words into the penal colony of a poem and hope that
hoffen, daß sie, obwohl sie nicht dorthin gehören, wenigstens hier
though they do not belong there they can at least learn something
etwas lernen, etwas Leichtes.
while they're there, something easy. But life is hard. The great,
important sight of it has to come from somewhere! Yes, of course,
I give my words free rein. Even the most inconspicuous word has
still learned how to say hello. I thank it politely. There's at least
one thing the writer needs to understand: that his life has two
sides, a bad side and a good side; two places, a place to sit and a
place to stand; and two classes, first but also wretched fourth.

IT'S A CAUSE OF CONCERN TO ME, since I don't want anyone
Ich möchte, was in mir
to see what I know just by looking at me. I want to know that
verwahrt ist, nicht bewahrt wissen.
what's in me will not outlast me. I have a good supply of myself

23

but it doesn't make me any bigger. Why should memory be death? Please, it can overwhelm a person, yes, but mostly it's just gentle and good to us. It was always different than we thought when we thought. The difference between sleep and death is the dream. And since we often forget our dreams, we naturally have often enough been dead. And? Did it hurt? No, not a bit! All right, so I'll happily die one day and take my leave with pleasure from this sick, weak, hope-poor, fear-rich world so that I can rest from all uncertainties and hardships in the good, dear, refreshing grave. Nonetheless, protect yourself for as long as I live from the protection of my words! Wait, I prefer to doff my hat before someone knocks it off my head! If you traverse these words you will run right into my inflamed, wide-open eyes trying to follow you. Sleep, in any case, wastes you away since you can't fall back on ardent contemplation of what has been so carefully protected. Why, then, should one protect oneself from something that escapes the stronghold of memory anyway? Memory is a hardware store where writers try to help themselves to something for free until all of the suffering falls on their heads because they pulled the bottommost plank out of the pile first. So now I garb myself in delicate absent-mindedness and no one can ask anything of me now, I'm dreaming, or temporarily dead at the moment. Alas I will know which one only after I have woken up and the weather has tempted me outside or not. Staying in my room doesn't mean I'm dead. Having been well-regarded at one time doesn't mean I wasn't dead. To put it another way: That I'm well-regarded today for a change might mean that I'm already dead, since on the whole the artist goes unnoticed during his lifetime unless he's a bad person or leaves something wanting in some other way – it can't be much, since he uses everything he wants for himself right away. He does almost always use and fetch the empty words himself. Oh, how hard it turns out to be to observe the good in every circumstance. Whenever I want, by the way, I can take back the furious look I've trained my face to have and can set other looks upon its rails. Sometimes the difference between life and death is so small that it's only a matter of whether someone writes in his spare time or writes on his spare time. He can succeed in the latter provided he remained alone and unobserved during the period granted him above and beyond his lifetime and

is not paged through unawares with one hand and beaten black and blue with the other.

NOW I'M LEAVING THE BUILDING. I will reach myself soon and nevertheless still be dead, right on time, if I hurry. I was right dead on time and could not admire this gentle and pure view of the world any more. In making the most cheerful of all possible faces I may in fact be supremely solemn and conscientious, and when I seem to be nothing but gushy and loving I am actually a solid, respectable expert. The attendant has just this minute told me: Good! For the time being you may withdraw, so that you can continue your nice little walk. *Sprechen ist, wenn die Stille endlich still ist.* Speaking is when silence at last falls silent. When the silence rings, please pick me up! Then you'll have one single listener on the line over which will come a voice saying: Who am I? Answer, please, so that one human being can finally come into being! So that the silence, brought to term by the whole world and all its things, can finally nurse and silence its children, so that they in turn will not open their mouths and grow loud. And so that nothing even worse will come into being: a being brought into its own through language and drowning out this wonderful silence by speaking too soon. So. Earth and Heaven flow and fall, run together and collapse, surging over each other like lightning in a blurrily shimmering mist-image. Chaos begins, order and the hierarchies vanish. He is shaken, he struggles to stay conscious; he succeeds. And then he confidently continues his walk.

THE HISTORY OF LITERATURE is full of ridiculous and tragic stories. Still, few are more tragic than the story of Robert Walser. For the last thirty years of his life he was sent away to live in a mental hospital and for almost the whole of that time he wrote nothing. No rest without motion, and motion – walks with Carl Seelig, and also alone – was allowed. Still, he often took them unwillingly, refused to bring his key; he had to, and wanted to, work in the institution sorting peas, folding tin-foil, gluing together paper bags. No special treatment for the former writer, no matter what! Fear, in fact, of a room of his own. He preferred to live with others! In ten-bed rooms would be best. The writer should finally get down to business and express himself!

But even when the way that leads outside is blocked, that doesn't mean you want to stay stuck inside yourself just because you have to. The beautiful, rich inner life of the writer, and he refuses to give it to us! Hides his light under a bushel when it isn't even his, it belongs to us all! This Robert Walser is one of those people who do not mean themselves when they say 'I'. It is true that he never stops saying 'I', but it's not him. Like the music of late Schubert, or Schumann: mouldering away without really meaning it. Walser sees what everyone sees. And he shows us his tools for taking up what he sees. He does this and that but, as Jürg Laederach said of him, he is like a buyer who studies the price list not because he wants to know what things cost but because he knows he will have to endure not being able to buy anything. No receipts are written up. The grand total comes out to nothing.

There the writer lies, dead in the snow, his hat has fallen from his head and lies next to him but still appears in the photograph. The title of this play – in German *er nicht als er*, literally 'he not as he' – has been put together from the syllables of his name but it doesn't add up to a whole or a meaning: Rob-er-t not as Wals-er, *er* not as *er*, he not as he; in translation too, -er- not -al-er, Her Not All Her. No one. Everything. Of his – most of this text, too, is from him.

Afterword:
In the Penal Colony

Reto Sorg

ELFRIEDE JELINEK's play *Her Not All Her (on/with Robert Walser)* is a strikingly original encounter with Robert Walser's life and work. It takes its place in what is now a tradition of tribute, and yet it demands to be read as an encounter not only with Robert Walser but also with the Walser Myth – a myth that has been generated by the numerous tributes to him, by the 'buzz' that surrounds him and his work. The title – in German *er nicht als er*, literally 'He Not As He', formed out of the sounds of Robert Walser's name – announces Jelinek's fundamental concerns: this is to be a text on and with Walser, in which he appears, but not as himself. We are led to expect not the identification of, or with, a person, but a reflection on the modes and forms of the Walser buzz; not 'he' is to take shape here, but someone/something else. To the extent that 'Robert Walser' is invoked, it is as an absent figure, personified in the rhetorical sense of achieving presence in his own writing and in the writing of others. The title, which at first seems merely playful, is revealed upon closer inspection as a manifesto for the play itself. (The title in English translation, preserving the play on Walser's name, adds another level: the text comprises the words of Jelinek, but not only of her, or of Walser, or of the translator.)

Jelinek's most obvious originality is that she has written a literary text following its own unconventional laws. The form stands out, as does the tone: a sometimes grating mixture of bathos and brittle irony familiar from her other works. For English-language readers, probably familiar with Jelinek's reputation as a strident feminist rather than through her work as a playwright or through her engagements with writers of the past, the whole project may come as something of a shock; the link to her oeuvre being that she sees Walser as non-self-identical, a player with, or victim of, different voices.

When it comes to the heaped-up juxtapositions of different styles, themes, and motifs that give Jelinek's text its stubbornly idiosyncratic character, she is in good company, since Walser's style too is unorthodox, ironic, hybrid, associative, and comic. Jelinek does write more cuttingly than Walser, who tends to remain remarkably moderate and proper. Her poetic emphasis proceeds from a fundamentally political position that is reflected in the form of her text – a form that makes it intractable, even rebarbative. The Swedish Academy, when awarding Jelinek the

Nobel Prize in Literature in 2004, stated that together with high literary quality her work levels a social critique: it praised 'her musical flow of voices and counter-voices in novels and plays that with extraordinary linguistic zeal reveal the absurdity of society's clichés and their subjugating power'. Especially in Austria, Jelinek's home country and the object of her deeply felt love and hate, it was big news, even a scandal, that the highest honour a writer can receive had been bestowed on a woman whose works – including *Women As Lovers* (1975), *Wonderful, Wonderful Times* (1980), *The Piano Teacher* (1982), *Lust* (1989), *The Children of the Dead* (1995), *A Sports Play* (1998) and *In the Alps* (2002) – contained such ferocious and outspoken descriptions of the sexist violence and latent fascism in Western democracies.

Jelinek (born in 1946 in Mürzzuschlag in south-east Austria) shares with Robert Walser (born in 1878 in the Swiss city of Biel) a predilection for structures and themes that subvert dominant ideas and familiar turns of phrase. They both delight in contradiction, and to that end make use of the spoken word in a style simulating speech, which Walser himself called his 'chatty tone'. In Jelinek, the colloquial tone comes to the fore as a result of the theatricality and gesturality that have marked her work from the beginning. Jelinek was a trained concert organist, and the musicality of her language, along with an unmistakable affinity for pop-culture, explode from her debut novel of 1970, *wir sind lockvögel baby!,* with its ironically mismatched fragments taken from various media and everyday life. Her preference for performance is also evident from the fact that she has written primarily for the theatre since the 1980s.

The present play, devoted to Robert Walser, is worlds removed from classical prose. It may give the impression of being a short story, but the subtitle and initial stage-direction make clear that it is composed as a spoken-word piece for multiple voices not clearly assigned to defined characters. What the characters say does not generate any strict plot or action, rather it forms a tangle of voices, a polyphonic language-cloud in which Jelinek's own voice(s) cut across, overlay, multiply, dissolve, and counteract Walser's voice(s), always also speaking about, with, through, to, from, and against itself (or themselves). Even as Jelinek makes every effort to remain at cross-purposes with the tradition of praise and panegyric, her text is emphatically a homage to a writer she loves and respects. At the same time, she tries to do the impossible: by claiming to speak not only about but *with* a dead writer, she makes failure into one of the guiding principles of her project. The desire for this kind of dialogue is as futile as is the attempt to speak the other writer's words as her own.

There exists a tradition of writing about Walser, which started while he was still alive (Christian Morgenstern, Hermann Hesse, Robert Musil, Franz Kafka, Walter Benjamin), which has since grown into an international chorus (Christopher Middleton, Susan Sontag, Roberto Calasso, William H. Gass, W. G. Sebald, Enrique Vila-Matas, J. M. Coetzee, John Ashbery, Giorgio Agamben, Rivka Galchen, Mikhail Shishkin, Ivan Vladislavić and others), and which has been extended into other media (Percy Adlon, Fischli/Weiss, the Quay Brothers, João César Monteiro, Mark Wallinger, Rosemarie Trockel, Stray Ghost, Thomas Schütte, Tacita Dean, Billy Childish, and more). In both content and dramaturgy, Jelinek's play is directed towards the image, or myth, of Robert Walser that has been produced over the years by these and other artists: Walser as naive genius who used his writing to reveal his existential position, whose career fell apart almost before it got started, who entered an insane asylum despite being sane, and who gave up his passion in order to live out the remainder of his life silenced as a writer – 'I came here not to write but to be mad'; Walser as the man found dead in the snow on Christmas Day by playing children, with an initially modest readership that has steadily grown until it now includes many of the most prominent writers and artists of our time. Jelinek's play is polyphonous, ambivalent, and provocative, although her afterword does make unambiguous enough claims. It subjects the Walser myth to literary defamiliarization, yet it also builds upon and furthers that myth, portraying Walser as the self-sacrificing artist who pays for his work with his life.

The play was premiered on August 1, 1998, directed by Jossi Wieler. Although often seen as difficult, it has been staged many times since, most recently in 2012 at the Deutsches Theater in Berlin. It is almost impossible to tell when any given utterance has Jelinek speaking directly or when she is quoting texts by or about Walser, since the voices and languages intertwine, overlap, and blend together. Nor is any solution offered to the tension

that arises from this stretto of perspectives. The play obstructs
the possibility of a cathartic outcome; Jelinek's voices are more
like a menacing choir that falls silent only when the play ends and
'silence at last falls silent'. It is as though the voices were echoes
of the unsettling voices that Robert Walser heard and described as
his 'sickness in the head'.

Who speaks? This question returns insistently in modernity, and
Jelinek addresses it when she writes, about Walser: 'Now who
does the writer mean by himself?' (The German, like the English,
contains both meanings: when alone/when he says 'myself'.) Yet
her play invokes more than merely the instability of the authorial
self, since it suggests that literary self-expression is not just a means
of self-definition and emancipation but also the expression of an
internalized obligation to confess, that is, to speak the whole truth
and nothing but the truth, first and foremost about oneself. But
those from whom such confessions are demanded find themselves
threatened with the loss of freedom; they monitor and punish
themselves. What Jelinek's play highlights is that the act of literary
confession, striving for self-determination, is always also an attempt
to free oneself from just this obligation to have any identity at all.

Robert Walser's work constitutes one of the great efforts in
modern literature at defining the self on purely its own basis. It
postulates that the writer fundamentally needs to proceed from
him- or herself – that writers cannot abstract out from themselves,
or from their immediate circumstances of living and writing.
Along with Kafka, Walser was one of the key writers who made
the twentieth century the age of autobiographical writing. By
turning their own artistic activity into their central object of atten-
tion, both produced astonishing works, such as in Kafka's case his
Diaries or in Walser's The Robber, two texts that attained conven-
tional book form only after their respective authors' deaths. Both
of these self-documentations not only testify to the experiences
of a single historical person, but also reflect the specific conditions
and possibilities of an identity mediated through literature.

What grounds Walser's work in reality is his stoic view of his
own life as a writer, where a writer is seen not as someone who
invents bold fictions but as one who turns his everyday personal
life into his subject. When he writes about himself ('Walser on
Walser' is the title of a late prose piece), Walser the writer is

cultivating Walser the writer as his literary material. He uses episodes from his own biography, offers perceptions and reflections anchored in the narrating and narrated self, and makes the context and act of writing into his theme; the overlap between the real person and the fictional character becomes the vanishing point of his work. Hence Walser himself contributed to the Walser myth. This is the starting point for Jelinek's play. She portrays Walser as someone who transposed his life into his work, to the point of self-sacrifice – someone who as it were dissolved himself into language, disappeared as a person, and turned into what he had written. Her play helps clarify why Walser has become an icon of modern literature: he invented himself in the act of writing and at the same time made himself disappear. By the end of the play, 'Robert Walser' is like a ghost, impossible to grasp despite his omnipresence.

Jelinek's play is a dialogue with a terribly exposed and almost other-worldly artist figure. Her own voice accompanies the voice of another, a kind of soul mate conversing with her and whom she wants somehow to preserve through her own words. At issue is what it means to communicate, to walk the same path, to hope that one is not alone, to admit the fear that perhaps one cannot express oneself in language at all. Jelinek's play reiterates what Walser's work too reveals: that along with and inseparable from the pleasure one takes in expressing and dramatizing oneself there is also a shame of language, which manifests itself in both a desire for discretion or retreat and in the urge to fall silent or disappear. The 'penal colony of a poem' mentioned in Jelinek's play – in the original, 'Strafkolonie einer Dichtung', literally the penal colony of poetry, or of a literary text or act of creative writing – is thus a place where every word made into literature is interrogated and forced to attest to its meaning. This idea, formulated by Jelinek about and with Walser, recalls Kafka's laconic summary in his story 'In the Penal Colony': 'It was as it had been in life; no sign of redemption could be seen'. If literature no longer offers redemption for Jelinek either, it nonetheless offers (as it says in her play) the possibility that words can 'learn something' and be given 'free rein'. For Jelinek as for Walser, writing neither offers total redemption nor is it the site of a complete breakdown; rather it is a profane way to herald, through failure, the cheerful messenger of resistance.

Translated by Damion Searls

A note on the images

The paintings reproduced in this cahier are from the series *Heads*
by Thomas Newbolt, about which art historian Martin Gayford
has written:

> In his newest series of pictures, Newbolt has painted faces and
> figures which are not done from models and not really from
> imagination either. You could say he found them in the dark.
> Most of them are done when there's almost no light left. He
> describes the struggle when the conscious intention is dull,
> the painting gets into an unconscious area and is in danger of
> getting lost, that's when he will do anything to save it. When
> the light fades, Newbolt knows exactly where each colour is,
> moving like a machine at dusk, coming over to the picture with
> a brush and putting the paint down where he thinks the nose
> is, because he can't really see.
>
> Talking about the series, Newbolt has said that 'the
> face must contain at least the possibility of happiness and
> unhappiness, thought and not-thought'.
>
> A few years ago Lucian Freud made some amendments to
> notes on painting he had written in 1954, and the main point
> he wanted to add was that, in the intervening half-century he
> had realised that painting is all about paint. Thomas Newbolt's
> working methods are quite unlike those of Freud – who
> invariably worked from life – but this attitude he does share.
> His paintings too are all about oil paint, and the discoveries
> that can be made with it.

COLOPHON

THE CAHIERS SERIES · NUMBER 18
ISBN: 978-0-9569920-4-8

Printed by Principal Colour, Paddock Wood, on
Neptune Unique (text) and Chagall (dust jacket).
Set in Giovanni Mardersteig's Monotype Dante.

With grateful thanks to Marie Donnelly
for her generous support.

Series Editor: Dan Gunn
Associate Series Editor: Daniel Medin
Images: Thomas Newbolt
Design: Ornan Rotem

Text: ©Elfriede Jelinek, 2012; afterword: ©Reto Sorg,
2012; translations: © Damion Searls, 2012; images:
©Thomas Newbolt, 2012; courtesy of the artist's
representatives: Piano Nobile Gallery, London.

Damion Searls has translated writers including
Proust, Rilke, Nescio, Thomas Bernhard, Hans
Keilson, Christa Wolf, and Robert Walser. He is a
Guggenheim Fellow and lives in New York City.
His translation of *Her Not All Her* won the Austrian
Cultural Forum Translation Prize.

Reto Sorg is the director of the Robert Walser
Center in Bern, Switzerland, and teaches at
the University of Lausanne. He has published
extensively on topics in nineteenth- and twentieth-
century literature and art.

CENTER FOR WRITERS & TRANSLATORS
THE AMERICAN UNIVERSITY OF PARIS

SYLPH EDITIONS, LONDON | 2012

THE AMERICAN
UNIVERSITY 50
of PARIS YEARS

center for writers and translators

SYLPH
EDITIONS

www.aup.edu · www.sylpheditions.com